AF347300

RLFPA
EDITIONS
RLPOETRY.ORG

Poems
by

SHALIM M HUSSAIN

Editor's Choice
RL POETRY AWARD 2017
National (India) Category

CONTENTS

A Brief Introduction

My mother is blood relative of Khairunnessa
Who had the temerity to overstep the threshold
Of her outhouse the night she gave birth.
The storm, waiting under an arum leaf
Swept her away and smeared
Her kidneys on betelnut trees;
They named her son Toofan Ali

My father was sperm of the sperm of
The sperm of jokers. A saint swam across
A river and proclaimed, 'Where there's water
There's fish'. 'Here's a coconut, master' they said.
He cursed their jute with nude caterpillars,
Them with thirst
And the river with perennial pregnancy.

Poetry will Belong

Mud will roll with pigs in poetry
Poetry will be a *jugalbandi*
Of Shikhar and spittle
Poetry will whistle through gap teeth
Dodge hate in bullet time
Borrow Diana's bracelets
Poetry will accept a chainsaw
And get cut to size like *segun* planks

Poetry will be *dadi's* cracked hands
Poetry will be turmeric caught in the cracks
And the old key she used to scoop it out
Poetry will be Mobil, poetry will be grease
Poetry will be a sackful of *bhoosa*
Poetry will be a grenade and
Burst into pieces of mist
Like simal pods

Poetry will be instant
Coffee with two pellets of Sugarfree.
Poetry will be the calendar of Taj Hotel
Poetry will be kupta, sick-kabab and libhaar
Poetry will be coconut husk and *dhuna*
Poetry will be the *chuur-chuur*
Of mosquitoes frying on an electric racquet
Poetry will be a dead lizard Feviquiked to the wall
Poetry will be eyelashes left in the sink

Poetry will be the fifth passenger
On a seat meant for four
On a tempo to Azara
Poetry will bear a knee to the crotch

Poetry will be a sheaf of *masur* dal
Cracked on baked earth by the lady with betel leaf lips
Poetry will be peas left to dry
On an empty Mama-Bhanja rice bag
In a bachelor's kitchen
Poetry will be NehaBhasin's loneliness

Poetry will learn its *aukaat*
Ma kasam, poetry will belong

Nana's New Clothes

One monsoon morning when he was ten,
Nana was granted his first set of new
Clothes- a vest and a lungi.
After a decade of nakedness
And his father's converted rags.
"I laughed and I cried", he is said to have told
His four daughters decades later.
"I paraded in them once and blessed them up for Id".
That white vest and that white blue lined lungi.
One monsoon morning when he was ten,
Nameless felled Nana's elder sister
Three fallen teeth and a hundred stories older
They didn't have the coins for a two meter shroud.
They planted her that rainy day
They buried her in that white-blue dream.
"And my rainy mouth"
Nana is said to have told ma and her sisters,
"Screamed shamelessly".

Nana- Maternal grandfather
Lungi or longyi- Long loose skirt worn by men.
Nameless- An euphemism for cholera.

15th August 1947

My grandfather woke up at four, maybe five
And shook the bamboo pillars

Reassured by coins jingling in the stem cavity
And the absence of a tunnel's mouth on the mud floor

He plucked a steel blade from the wall
And trimmed his corns. His oldest daughter

Cried. My grandmother freed the milk-soaked Edge of her sari
from under a heavy arm.

My other grandmother splashed a cup of mustard oil
On the cows' udders, my other grandfather

Dusted a cap and walked to the mosque. Late in the morning he ate
Rice and boiled potatoes, or picked a jumpy fish from the pot and

Threw it in the fire. Grandfather returned angry,
Grandmother turned wild ferns on the pan,

Fried onions, two crushed garlic cloves and half a dried fish
All afternoon the two men separated by a river planted

The same rice saplings, all afternoon the two women
Dusted dried stalks of the same masoor

At night they ate boiled potatoes, rice and
Went to bed after ten minutes of in and out-

One's bed jingled, the other held her pace
When they slept they all slept well. The next

Morning at marketplaces on either side of the river
They heard the news.

A Lesson in History

My grandmother's only fear was that she would lose her
children.
Have many children, she said
To anyone willing to listen
If you have one child
And if that one child dies, what will you live on?
She and Dada did a good job.
Fertile for thirty five years until menopause
She had fifteen children
Four of whom didn't survive childhood
And whom she rarely mourned.

Like all sensible children of the river
She made peace and pancakes for the
River and the tremors.

In '50
When the earth shook like a bull on heat
She prayed to old forgotten gods
She prayed to the energies of the universe.
When the ground beneath her bedstead cracked
And spat out boiling fish, she steeled her nerves.
Stood on her doorway and waited for the wriggling and
writhing to end.

She waited on the doorway for flesh to fall off the bones,
Then collected the dried heads,
Hung them on the jute reed wall
Beside a poster of pink roses
And a framed embroidered handkerchief
Passed a thread through the spines and made a cummerbund
Wore it for the rest of her life

Until almost four decades later
dying of a rot in her ovaries
With her children witnessing the wasting
She knew she had
At last defeated the earthquake
And broke the thread.

Standing by Abba's Grave

I have seen the sun stewing in a pond
I have seen the patience of ripples
Seen them crouch at the pond's edge
And pounce on a water insect's feet.
I have seen reeds stand as sentinels and
Hold back what they can
Their hips swaying and the sun in the sky smiling.
I have seen palm trees rise golden from the bank
look this way, then that
And throws its seeds at my feet
I have woken with muddy orange mud at my feet
Orange fish in my hands
And seen my orange backed mother
Stands before my Abba's orange grave.

I walked hard on the mud
Itburpep and swallowed my feet
Fish wriggled free
Fell on the filmy orange skin
Of the muck
And brushed my toes as they swam away
Pain pulled at my heart, forget-me-nots tugged at my lungi.
I left them both behind and fell panting on the ground-
Naked in body, naked in mind
At the feet of my creator
As I was presented to her.

Ma walked one step, I crawled two
Grass flowers died at her toes,
Died at my chest
Her feet and my lips met at the edge
And together we peered

Into the landslide of Abba's grave

Mud weights weighed down white bones
Bamboo nets on bamboo staves lay rotten
Ma and I look at brown bone marrow
Mixed with brown mud
And we can't differentiate.

Fifty years of existence, five years of death
Held down by five handfuls of earth
In a five foot hole
And orange footprints on the mud
Speak to me in fox-tongue,
"I was here".

Ma lies flat and pokes at the bones
They don't combine and arise

And as I turn to her to say, "Forget it",
The pond fills my mouth with wet wind
I choke and the words remain unsaid.

The lord looks from below,
His bride looks from above and they can't meet
Her flat bosom, like a punctured pimple,
Entices him no more

Darkness sublimates into the air
A spray of raindrops drizzle upon us four
Four dark creatures around a hole
Three creators, one creation-
One rotten, one rotting,
One watching them rot,
One paddling the wheels of fate.

Golluckgunj

After a long ride down a road newly raised
And porcupined against the river
We unload our cameras on a rice field half-India half-
immigrant
 Its two weeks past the 26th of January-

And they are celebrating.
The rain came first and let me tell you it was cold, cold-
We had to postpone the Republic. His lungi is muddy, his ganji
crusted with
Sweat. Looks like the map of Bangladesh, he laughs

Then asks if the camera is on.

I stand on the raised border- two endless lines of concertina
Four strings on each line, the space in between
Heaped with more coiled wire.
I wonder but don't ask if they are electrified.

The border policeman on his bicycle stops, eats his lunch on
the grass
He has never cycled across the lines.
The air from the other side filtered through the metal screen
should
But doesn't smell different.

I had more expectations
From my first international border, I guess.

There, on that raised mound
Where four lines of betelnut trees mark a rectangle
And still ripen every March, inside that was home.

Our phones catch the signal from the other side.

He feeds us country chicken and fish. We sit on his wife's
furniture
Five years old but the varnish still glossy. The false ceiling, an
old sari-could have been his late mother's. And the door I lean
against
Looks old, so old that it could be

The last remnant of the home across the lines.

Birth Certificate

The last time I arm-wrestled my father
He made me struggle
Against his strength
Against a granite palm-print
Against the bamboo knots on
His fingers
The familiarity of which I had
Almost forgotten.

And just when
I had almost brought him down
He gave one last push
I gave up.
His back on the floor,
His skin and the thin layer of concrete
Almost the same he asked
Son, how old am I?
Forty eight I said

They printed the same on his death certificate.

I protested: boys went to school late in the '50s
There were always the younger ones
To care for, the cattle to feed
The famine to survive.
My aunt opened her father's Quran
Against alif lam meem were the dates
Of her birth, the three after her that
Didn't survive and my father's

My plan to give my father a few more years
Came to nothing.

The Holy Cross

At the morning mass the good sisters taught us

How to make the holy cross.*In* on the forehead

The name of the mumbled as hand moves down

Father on the heart, *son* and *holy spirit* on left and right

Armpits. We didn't bother to notice that every *and the*

Passed criss-cross on our chest: straps binding holy armour

On our upper bodies. We grudged the Mallu boys their
Eucharist

And at the last amen ran to the mess for breakfast.

A Little Shopping for Father

Seven years before he passed,
The old man
Thrust a hundred rupees in my hand
And whispered that I and I alone
Should buy the ten metres of plain white cloth
For my father, his eldest son.
Someone scolded him,
You fool, they said,
How can you make him do this?
But Dada was not at fault.
He didn't own his mind
And worse, he didn't own anyone's trust

Some kind soul took the blood money from me
But later in the afternoon when the burial was over,
I walked between the mosque and the hardware store
A polythene bag wrapped around my brain
And a passing stranger asked if I was hungry.

He walked me to a sweet store,
Almost gloated as I sat silently
My cheeks puffed with too much crying
My lips burning with sugar syrup.
The stranger left me his handkerchief
And money to pay for the meal.

I Loved You

I loved you between a hill and a river.

Before the planned encounter
At a hospital cafeteria
Where caught between the smell of phenyl
And what you joked was treated human flesh in the chicken
patty
I tried looking into your eyes but skied down
The sharp rise of your cheek and
First felt in the fluffy sweet of your shampoo
The softness of your hair.

At JB's
First a pizza, then three cups of coffee,
Then when our money ran out
The owner asked if we could kindly order something else
Or clear the seats for customers
Snorting diesel fumes
And tapping their feet at the door.

In my head we were already
Walking down Nilomoni Phukan path
Our fingers engraved in each other's palms.
The road, curved like a lizard's tail between G S Road and the
zoo,
Woke and flicked us to Dispur
We fell before the gates of a new empire
And slowly rose in the air
On the city's first escalator.

I loved you at the Regional Science Center.
Under the protective gaze of a dinosaur

I left my hand on your thigh
And cart-wheeled around the garden
Then said I had a secret
That could only be whispered.
Caught you half-aware, half smiling
And breathed the secret on your lips

Kissed you at full speed down the Ulubari flyover
A passing trucker smiled, *'Dheeredheere'*
The prophet was merciless
At a speed breaker our teeth clashed
Your lip bled
But it was okay.
Kissed you luck before the changing room in B Borooah
College
Dusk had fallen; hasna-henna was in the air
My hand around your waist
And that was the wisest thing to do.
Kissed you on the rocks at Sankardev Kalakshetra
Before the open theatre was laid
And in Tezpur University before Jyotiprasad drew the
blueprint.

In a bus conductor's cracked voice
I asked for you
At Adabari, Maligaon, Kamakhya, Bharalumukh,
Fancy Bazar, Panbazar, Dighalipukhuri.
There was a drivers' strike
Alone I walked up a hill
Found you under a radio tower at the medical college,
I grabbed the railway tracks
Tore the city's veins
Tied you to my back
Wrapped you up in Guwahati

And carried you through laburnums- golden, red and pink

We ran away to
Marine drive with Anirudh Karnick
Hid under his wet sheets at the International Hostel room
Of Delhi University
I loved you in the back lawn of Jamia
On a park bench while Kharingpam blew smoke rings and
Laughed at the audacity of a bearded man
Fondling a girl in a burqa.

At Patna I loved you in a hotel bathroom with a leaking tap
And a rusty razor blade
While the city lolled outside mad with reefer smoke
At Gaya we drove past cacti and the soul of the Faguniriver
Spread out to dry on the sand
A human family shielded a sow and her piglets
In their shared household
And an old man appeared
Of discarded paper plates, beer bottles,
A thousand year old Hanuman scratched on the belly of a
rock,
His face painted with yesterday's *gulal*,
Guided us up Asoka's footsteps carved in stone.
I loved you in the darkness of Sudama's cave
Our eyes blazed in the flash of camera phones
And the writing on the wall burned with devotion

I loved you with purple rain
And fell on my back
A sheet of paper shivering on my hands and wrote
You a final love song
Furious the thoughts came unbridled, unbroken
I sat on my knees and scrawled,

Then cast the pages aside and proclaimed,
'I am the Jimi Hendrix of writing.'

A harpoon pierced my cousin's back
And poked it's fingernail out of his chest.
Before he was buried, people wondered how a tiny trickle of
blood
Under his breast pocket could kill him.
They half-accused me.
The mob scaled our walls
Stood on the rafters
Checked if our 'hired killers from across the river'
Were there.
Among my father's old books, rat droppings
And the husks of empty betel nuts, they found no conspiracy.
Yet they waited outside
And my mother, aunts, brother, sister, cousins
Locked themselves in
His soul entered their food.
The dal grew thinner
The curries lost meat and fish
For days they ate gourds from the vegetable garden
With a single egg
Carefully placed between celebration and blandness.

On the phone
Rambling while escaping half asleep
Through Mukalmua, Nalbari, Barpeta, Howly, Barpeta Road,
Sorbhog, Kalgachia
My head banging against the bus window
My temples swelling with blood
I finally confessed my love: I had little to lose.
I passed the River Oufura
And my father, naked except for his underpants

Shivering under the water,
Scribbling on his notebook
His pen burnt to cinders by the
Fires of 1983
Raised his head
Pink hibiscus floated around his head.
He stared his disapproval.

I loved you in Majerchar
For three months in the solitary confinement
Of my mother's sister's husband's granary
You asked if the clucking in the background was hens.

I loved you behind a public notary's desk at the Guwahati
High Court
Before a blast threw a hammer at my ribcage.
Caught my breath at the corner of Ambari masjid
Caught sight of army trucks moving shyly
Like a fresher on high heels or
A performer on stilts
Trying as best as they could
To hide shame, incapacity and the disgusting smell of burnt
flesh
Under a blue tarpaulin

I ran to Cotton College and
As ground concrete and molten rubber settled,
Loved you under William Sudmersen's bust.

I threw you on *Jejuri*
And watched you crawl
Your feet caught between the sticky lines
Then walked a dead grass road from
Anundoram Barooah Hostel

To the Guwahati railway station.
Spat on the ground.
Straw, phlegm and earth joined hands and formed Gods
I could have fallen flat on the ground and prayed but
The bombs went off again
Cycle rickshaws jumped twenty feet
The pan-sellers grew wings and flew
I lost faith.

I loved you at Bharalumukh
Where the blackness of the drain
Met the cheerful grey of the river,
I worshipped you with coconut water at Church Gate,
With vodka at Cotton College
Christened the cocktail 'Brahmaputra on the rocks'
Then stood half-drunk at the Dispur Secretariat
As they tore shame off a young woman's body
And made her run naked through the streets.

It was 2007, you were depressed.
I took you to Chandubi
After the river changed its course
Trees a thousand years old
Stood defiant under the lake
I loved you in the clear water
Between the roots of history.
We swam by your office on the Jorpukhuri pond
Sank slowly into the Dighalipukhuri bog
I loved you behind Nilamani Phukan's house
Where a thin stream crawled out of a rock's butt-crack.

I loved you up the winding Gandhi mandap path,
Mystified by your hatred
For red meat

Then bought you a rose and before you left me
Confused
Like a lamp-post in the middle of the market
Sulphur burning in 100 watt bulbs,
Men sweating all shades of masculinity and
Fish intestines clogging the drain,
You leaned and whispered in my ear, 'I love you'
I held the rose's stalk in my hand and wondered.

I loved you at the gynecologist's
Where the doctor said, glancing at me, then you, then me
That your ovaries
Had swollen to the size of duck's eggs.
You laughed, you were luckier than the girl
Who loved anal sex but had hemorrhoids.

I swam on a pomfret's belly,
Rowed towards you on a sliver of raw mango.
I loved you before star anise, coriander seeds, cumin, mace,
nutmeg
Before biryani recipes, haleem
I stole you from engineers, travel bloggers and the Indian
bureaucracy
Hid you under hyacinth, wood ducks' eggs.
Poetry shaved his head,
Tuned a guitar
And in a voice strong, elastic, durable
He taught you all about finding lost boats
And tethering them to the shore.
He stole you from me.

Beside the Brahmaputra what remained
Of my heart broke like a cloud
The rains failed, the earth cracked

The hills melted like jaggery.

I hated you enough to carry a note in my pocket
And loved you enough to throw it
Not me over the Gandhi mandap cliff.
I allowed myself the silence of a sparrow
Perched Batman-like on the iron palm of an incomplete high-
rise
The languidness of an addict and the
Oblivion of a grasshopper
I loved you before boyhood, spectacles and my only cardigan
Before beards, chewing tobacco and machismo.
Before blasphemy.
I loved you before time.

At Anwar's Wedding Reception, December 2009

I fear gatherings,
Said the girl at the wedding party.
The howls and screams of new children,
laughter,
The sweat and dust trickling down
Swirls of bamboo spears
Into cauldrons of flesh.
Yellowed wounds of cauliflowers,
The flight of worms of ash.
The wishing and greeting,
And silent flirting in corners,
Old men clustered around dead stories,
The blaze of red saris,
The whiteness of beards and caps
And rice bubbling in mad milk
Pyramids of chopped timber,
The shit and pee of overnight guests
The brownness of burnt gravy.
The glass eyes of perverted fish.
And fistfuls of salt
Showered in benediction.
Since…

Since?

Since His last feast.

City of Dead Fairies

You will be a stranger in
The city of dead fairies, she said
How could I tell her that all this drifting
Between minds and lands
Had made me one long ago
At home, at the sheepman's last song
'Hai re hai, the toga's butt is red'
As it flapped away,
I could only see its blackness
Trailing against the winter's white.
Stepping on sharp grass, my
Feet cut on the edges
And blood dewed out on the silver green edges.
When simal pods burst to release
The sima within,
I saw only dreams wafting
On feather backs.
My neighbour was a black water tank and
A row of betel nut trees
Until one evening I wandered into our common backyard
And as cobwebs settled on my hair
And one dry leaf grafted on my forehead,
Stumbled on the lichen on two old tombs.
Today my neighbour- a straw filled
Desert cooler hugs me tight when I pass.
Then as a strange pointy haired fairy of five
I tried to blow fog to match my uncle's cigarette tricks.
Today, I don't wait for seasons or fog.
And when I trudge my soul up the great mosque's steps
To cry 'prayer is better than sleep',
My voice vibrates against the wings of ghosts.
Then when the boatman anchored us on a sand bank,
And passed a sky of blue tarpaulin over our heads,

I smiled at two pairs of ancient teeth
Rolling up hope and damnation in a
Paper cylinder of weed.
Then sneaked out to see the river lashing and lashing again
On the nose of the boat
A nose so fair and warted with dark fear
As on an old woman's praying face.
Here, I stand in rolled up pants seeing the rain churn up streets
Into the whirpool of naked manholes.
Then pulling my feet away from its gargling,
Open my palm for flowers
Descending as soft as teardrops.

Anundoram Barooah Hostel 2006

Ft. Stuti Goswami

It burns her tongue a little
She gathers the frown on her eyelash
The wrinkle on her nose, the sharp intake of breath
On the puckered lips and
Blows it on the tea's skin
Milk and water shiver a little
Sweeten a little
Mist shades her eyes just a little
And she draws in her sari, draws in her legs
The goddess strikes an ungodly pose
The ghost on the top floor yawns
The boys emerge foaming at the mouth
It's six in the morning.

They… theyare already here
With their own weapons
And gunny bags
Their scythes are spears, bent in the end
Sharpened like bloody hockey sticks
They swing
A curve gracefulas a golf shot
The grass flies from its stalk
She stares long and slow,
Says, 'Each leaf sings a song of bereavement'

These men with strange names
Akkel, Daelbor, Khokshed, Fokkor
Names as exotic as Meluha and Amarkantak
Names like the wriggling of a snail lost
In a foghorn
And when they call their women it's like the

Beat of a metronome- Rahaton, Bahaton, Shahaton
Or the tap-tap-tapping of a woodpecker
The put-put-put of a chatak bird
Which lost its son and still roams the world looking for it

When they leave I look for them
Under tarpaulin sheets
On the footpaths
Where I hear they burn chicken legs, chicken hearts, chicken
skin
And all that's left after
Boneless chicken has been carved off for the luxury of hotel
guests
Transparent skin on chicken breasts
Lumps of chicken skin
And heads and ample amounts of offal
And where it is said they make wild love.
I look under the flyovers,
I lift the drapery of the Brahmaputra
And seek among the bones of Mughals, Pandavas and the
Maan
Under the policeman's baton

Stuti looks up dreamily. She says,
Words are grass.

The Sparrow and Jayanta

A sparrow fell off the eaves
A wingspan of sky
Crashed into the cracked floor.
Jayanta picked it,
Ran a thumb over its breast
And blew.
And a thousand ants cloistered in a speckled
wound
Scattered like cotton wisps.
One by one they bit his fingers
One by one he shook them down
One by one crunched under his naked feet.
As each ant soul rose up like a wish,
And buoyed the wings,
He spat on the wound.
Blind eyes healed, the blood wound sealed
The sparrow fanned ant souls into the wind
And flew.

Jayanta's flapping shawl saffroned
His hair matted,
His eyes closed, his wide smile…

Until the raven swooped down
A peepul tree and closed its ebony scissors
Around the sparrow's neck.
In one mid-flight thrust,
Snapped open the bird like a prayer book
Four wings in flight thrashed.
The raven drove its claws in and in…

Blood showered.
The ants at Jayanta's feet crawled back to life.

Dressing my Father

Fifteen years ago
And two days before the Panchayat elections,
Abba dressed
It was an odd ceremony
God knows why I remember it all.
He bathed in the open bathroom
His lungi on the bamboo wall

I carried his warm water.
Later when he was done
He walked into the house in a towel
Barely covering his thighs
His arms were white,
His feet were white
And white was all over his head
He had stopped dyeing his hair
He had let old age come in.

He made a mental note to buy some towels
While we waited,
Me my brother and my sister
To daub him in perfume
It was strange.
He stood and smiled
Smiled like a child.
We went through the briefcase that held
His books, his writing
And all his clothes
We finally found a vial of rose water.

He let me roll two cotton balls between
My thumb and forefinger

And tuck them behind his ears.
Gulam dipped an ear-bud, rolled it
On the lapel of his shirt,
Behind his buttons

It was so new and so discomforting
We were all shy.
Our father's body was taboo
Our father's body shamed us.
We never clung to him as children do.
When we met on the first day of the vacations
He shook our hands.
And on the last day he helped us comb our hair.
He turned us to gentlemen
Demarcated a space we should never cross.
And of course there was the other thing
The smell of stale tobacco
That followed him like Dog our dog.
The smell was strong, rough, unpolished.
He carried a tin container
Which opened both ways:
One half contained lime and the other tobacco.
The one's he shared his tobacco with
Were the ones he opened his private life to
Not his wife, not his children.

Except for Salma
Who was too little then
Too little to know that her father was an old man
For her he was a clothes hanger,
A swing, a horse
And anything she wanted him to be.
That morning she clung to his neck and went full banshee.

At the Counsellor's Office

Sir, she will tell you of the
time she saw
water swimming in a bottle

she will tell you
it was the best time
the air was wet, a sheet of paper
swinging
under her ceiling fan
and the water in the bottle shivering

she will tell you about
the breeze
stepping off the edge of her fifth floor terrace
then slicing the face
of her kitchen knife
and all that water
throbbing

there's one thing she won't say
because she doesn't know
at seven that night
a draught of winged ants
flooded our room
and draped our tube-light-
all except the one
that got in the bottle
and before it left,
set the water thrashing.

Saraswati Puja at Anundoram Barooah Hostel, Cotton College

Room 109.
Once a year, today, the unofficial storeroom
Realises its true identity.
Trunks and bedrolls of champion runners
Who have run away from festivals
Or ten months of unpaid dues
Are drawn out into other rooms,
Broken cricket equipment and deflated footballs
And yelps of joy rediscovered,
"My old jockey" or a long lost shoe and sometimes a book.
The windows jammed for a year need props to stay up.
Then green curtains are taken for washing or for the fire,
The treasure trove of ancient cupboards are thrown open
To a cascade of Illustrated weeklies and first edition novels
And the library secretary gets a 'puwali' to mop the floor.
In good tradition, the money allotted for 'intellectual and
aesthetic purposes'
Have long gone
Into buying the mess committee's text books.
Outside, 'Bangladeshis' that were chased out of the pavement
A week ago
Turn grim reapers
And swing the scythe over six months of grass.
The mess secretary pays Manik (more of an archive, less of the
head cook)
For tomorrow's special rations,
The auditor cooks his calculations,
The magazine secretary scouts for prospective poets
To finish a week's work in a day.
Hardship and stress but no worries.
Cotton is tradition's favourite step child.

It burns her at the fireplace but rocks her on its knee.
The ever-green roof of the hostel,
The cement coated reed walls,
The broken plaster on the floor repaired every decade,
The flower plants stunted behind iron gates,
The old tree under which herons drop their feathers,
The old flagpost-
They say the same thing.
A few times a year, Cotton sheds its glassy liberalism
And tradition walks in with her iron cane.
This time, she smiles
As values are polished and passed on.
The idol-makers tell a different tale-
"Biswakarma sells better than Saraswati."
But still press clay wisdom on Aai's straw face
And passionate nipples on her perfect breasts.
It's a sin to say, Aai forgive me,
But tomorrow your old self will be drowned
And a fresh one put in the library's dark corner, beside the old phone
To be fondled and caressed and kissed
By frustrated bookworms.
Today, the two water tanks are cleaned
And all underwear dried and removed from the clotheslines
Because when the sun shines eight tomorrow morning,
ARB gates will be opened
To a flurry of fairies.
"The loveliest girls study in Cotton college," HomenBorgohain will say again
As CG empties itself into the ARB grounds.
The 'puwali' will stare from behind half-opened doors,
Still wondering which clothes make him a man,
Seniors will walk up wondering how a glorious nine-yard rag
Can create butterflies.

And so will wonder other oglers from other hostels
And nostalgic old pass outs who can't be younger or ARBians
anymore.
The groups will break and clusters float about.
In the century old dining hall
Of sparrows, bad lighting, decayed walls and one running tap,
Aluminium topped tables will fill with paper plates
Of khicdi and Manik's antique pickles.
Couples will steal morsels amid glances; K-bond will smirk,
Manik will ruin appetites with his greasy smile
And Siddhu, dressed for once in trousers
Will sing of youth and loss.
No one will mind the snails on arum leaves
Or the drains overflowing with two-feet depths of decaying
rice
Just outside the walls.
But that's tomorrow.
Tonight, in ARB's literary room,
Beds will be pushed to sides, chairs will be piled
And on the floor hallowed by a million feet,
Tea and biscuits will flow
And cigarette butts multiply
As ten hands ache with calligraphy and painting
And snipping ribbons and carving thermocol
And mounting the wall-magazine on its moth-eaten stand
For tomorrow's competition.
The two monitors will lean on old wood bedsteads carved and
smoothed
And recarved with a thousand names.
At five in the morning when all is done,
They will dance under the faraway tubelight on the verandah
And shout, "Pusu, come out."
Pusu- the hostel superintendant with a politer real name
Will listen but sleep on.

And they, finally tired, will lie on the bits of paper and
cardboard and ribbon
And when the priest blesses each student under the glorious
February sun
Or when ARB wins the prize for the magazine,
They will be dragged out of dreamland.

The Snake and the Tree Frog

One day long long ago
A snake running away from hounds
Jumped over a hedge
Consigned half his tail to concertina
And fell before a tree frog.

His heart melted
And flowed out of his blinking eyes.
For her, he was just another snake.

She said hello
He said hi.
She swung from branch to branch
Her milk-green skin
Dropped like dew-drops on the leaves and
Vanished.
He stretched his arms, fell backwards on the grass
The hounds snapped behind the hedge
But life was sweet!

They met at social events
His voice dipped in the natural dandiness of snakes
Slithered down her skin
She, cautious like all frogs
Maintained a one-arm distance.

'Baby, let's make it work.'
'No, our species are incompatible.
Say, can I take you to an assembly of frogs?'
'I will behave, I won't eat them.'
'Doesn't change a thing.'
'You taste awful! Slimy, green, bitter!'
'Look who's talking!'
They shook hands and never met again.
We have both evolved now.
Though I still have the snake's bad eyesight
I see nineteen hundred miles away

The glimmer of moonlight
On her milk green back

She is too polite.
When she calls, she doesn't mind my hissing.
She doesn't tell me of my ancestor's dried tail
Fluttering on the hedge.
But this age still makes us two.
In my kiss she feels the forked tongue
In my touch, scales.
Like my father, I keep shedding skins
And remain the same snake.
She, fully changed from frog to woman
Tries, just tries.

On Loving Old Men

Television taught us that we could love our fathers
Life didn't.
No one and nothing taught us to love our grandfathers
Except distance
And distaste for the
Silly disaffection of my mother
Towards her father-in-law

It didn't help that Dada whimpered through the night
Like a baby
His whimpering was loud and constant
And like the two minutes of throat-clearing
In the microphone
Before *azaan*
It woke us all.

My grandfather saw visions
He saw half-dreams
I saw him up on his bed in the dark,
One hand on his mouth,
One on his nose
We shook him.
'Flies', he said, 'Flies all around.'
Flies so thick he could not breathe
He tried to pull up his shoulders,
cover his ears, shut their buzzing
He feared they would enter his nose and mouth
And stuff his foodpipe

He said the bull would gore him
We turned on the lights, gave him his glasses
Pretended to clear the air
He slept
But as I turned off the light
I alone saw his knees move to his chest
His hands move to his face.

Ma said that it was a shame
For a wife to die before her husband
Grandmother orphaned her husband
A decade before he was free
To lie naked on a plank of wood
For professionals to tear off his clothes,
Soap his body
And cocoon him in ten meters of white cloth
All the while gazing at their watches,
Looking at the sun and wondering

If they were too late.

Namaaz

I had to clean myself

But before the first drop from the nozzle fell,

The wetness of your tongue was on my palm

The rest was all ritual- hands and arms and face and feet

I tucked rose water in my ears

And pulled an old cap over my hair

But the few strands that stuck out were yours

Especially the one that ran down my cheeks.

I rolled up my pants and rolled out the mat

And on the velvet on the sheet, I could feel the underside of
your feet

When I turned west and announced I would offer him

My prayers, God knew I wasn't fooling him.

The Decaying Art of Lying

Is all one needs to master
And hide; for truth
Is simple, effortless-
In curricula a journey, in religion ecstacy
And for one who neither obeys nor seeks
Ethics do the trick. Lying is lace and liquorice
The slapping of rain on glass windows.

In truth one's earliest memory is a shadow
Of a mother and child flapping
Against a mud wall.
Open your eyes and it's a crusty baby
Under a layer of mashed hair and clay
And an open fire grabbing shadows and
Lashing them against the mud wall.
Somewhere there is laughter.

In truth one's father's bones have decayed
And there is nothing in his returning every night
Every night after fifteen years.
His face so changed
With a detachment so strong you can only ask
'How is your other family?'
Every night he stands outside the gates
And speaks his two words in a tone
You have forgotten but know
Is not his.

It's easy to know that things just are, to make peace but the
struggle
To say otherwise gives you what, hope?
Bear with my lies a little for truth will give you

Abstractions- a little time, a little space, the rare
Cosiness of history but I,
Will break you to bits and give you poetry.

Bright Night

I squat outside.
Sad scrotums of wild pota-
toes swing

I feel my cheek
The moon trickles down my piddle
I finger

My lips
On my neck a puff of moth
And I shiver

Away
From the tender touch
Of man.

Have you ever, just licked a Raisin?

Have you held it

      in

your mouth

and felt it swell to a

grape?

When Numbers turn Sentient

You speak their language, eat their food
You have both gone to the same schools
Visited the same places.
And yet when it happened,
You looked into the mouths of words
Studied their teeth
The colour of their tongues
Put test tubes in their bellies
CT scanned their brains
Prescribed caution against exertion
Medicines, care, proper nutrition.
Then sat them across the table and decided
Memoranda of understanding.
It is safe to assume that you know
All about words.

Now what do you do when a number
Frowns at you from a graph
A number you have never touched, smelt,
dipped your fingers in
Whom you know by sight, not by name
Who look all the same
What do you do when a decimal point reddens its eye
Or 8 gets hit, falls on its side
And stares with infinite hate
Or 1 leans forward and points
A finger
Or worse, sets a head on its shoulders
And becomes a word?
Right now it's fine.
Numbers have no mouths.

But numbers have eyes and skins.

What do you do when
Numbers turn sentient?

Your Name is Hussain & you are a Terror

Your name is Hussain and you are a terror
Your existence is fire and brimstone
Your laziness an unpinned grenade
Your steady silence an affront to a world stinking of sulphur

Your ignorance a sledgehammer in Palmyra.
Your partial deafness a cluster-bomb
Your measured protest ashower of pellets
Your joy at being more platypus than wood duck
More bat than bird
More cockroachthan dinosaur
An anomaly.

Every hair maturing on your chin
Every finger steady in suspense
Before hitting a keyboard
Bears witness.
TheDay of Judgmentwill not end
The night of recollection will come soon.

Your complacency is anthrax
Your quiet a salivating sword
Your name is Hussain and I declare you a terror.

Soft Underbelly

Meditations on the patch between my lower lip and chin that hurts every time I write a line which may not really belong in a poem but which I include simply because I love it- not the complete line (well, sometimes the complete line) but mostly some of the words (the way they sound, or just their shape beside a cursor going hmmm let's see let's see hmmm let's see let's see), thereby giving the poem a felling of pretentious self-seriousness without meaning anything remotely profound

    Kick me there and I am out

Essay on the most Memorable Day in my Life

I still remember the day
I offered a little girl on the bus
A seat on my knee
Only to realize that she was a midget
Well past twenty.

She stared through parted cherry lips
I was glad my father was sleeping
And my pride, newly born at fourteen
Slid down my belly.

Vomiting a Snake

Death by impaling on a bamboo staff is not rare enough
Enough children climb trees
Enough houses are guarded by bamboo fences
Enough children are left unguarded.
When Sokina died of three bamboo staves
Sinking through her back and
Protruding from her chest,
We didn't visit the family.
We visited them when her grandfather vomited a snake.

The news filled the village with panic.
It was a live writhing snake, they said,
Two-headed some said.
Stood on its tail and sprang from his throat they said.
And so Ma and we her children planned the trip.
We booked a rickshaw, awoke at dawn, packed a lunch.

As we got closer, we met people also going to see the old man
Or returning from the site.
With every hundred steps the story changed.
No, it was not a snake
But an unidentifiable long-bodied reptile
No, it was not a reptile
A creeper.

When we finally reached in the evening
Our clothes dusted all over
Our faces sticky with grime
What we saw was a jute-string like
Six inch long thin string.
Years of chewing betel nut can do that.
It had accumulated in his stomach
Only to be regurgitated today.
So much for myths.

Rani of Rajouri

When you wake at 6
There are things
You should expect of the rani of Rajouri-
Legs crossed, folded, fingers
Tangled in last night's party hair,
Eyes paring paper, cellophane,
Repeat gifts (for everyone knows
The queen's love of gun-metal),
The memory
Of a swirling in the head,
A walk to the washroom, a peek of a
Friend's bra and
Lips pressed with the pink
Of a few hours past twenty one.

The Poet at Connaught Place

By the time the poet calls to say that she might be late
Summer has come
Roads melt, mirages sit cross-legged
On corn cobs and
The big flag goes white.

She comes in what remains of saffron and green
Dips a snake in tarmac
Draws a fish-belly under her eyes
'A trick, a trick'
She pulls the edges of Rajiv Chowk

And makes you a paper tree
Plucks a sparrow, a parrot, a chopta from
Its leaves. Then
Birds on one shoulder, hair
Pulled from paddy fields

Dyed in peat and sunshine
On the other
She smiles a smile that's here
But not quite here
And orders mutton cutlets.

Dighalipukhuri*

One claw on a bar,
and crow
lifts the other to his lips
Blows the day's first puff.
His view races smoke through the fencing,
conductors spank buses -
'Dighalipukhuri.Dighalipukhuri.'

Long pond.

He stares at a chirping he can never touch,
at entwined buds,
and pigeons floating in air bubbles,
and lovebirds in love rows,
heads under wings.
His downy heart bleeds over the bliss beneath.

At home, his vulture
waits,
a spear in her hair and
a carcass in her beak.

Here he makes his day long,
sometimes swoops down and scoops up
beakfuls of love from the face of
Dighali.
Love like the blushes of hyacinths
skimmed behind boats.
The trees branded with Duryodhan's incense,
Bhanumati's anklets still tinkle under the
paddle-boats,
her turmeric and potfuls of milk

her wedding tears
and a few thousand years of love.
He will return to blow the night's last mists.

Walford

Walford stank
Of turpentine floors,
Sterile needles and the ridiculous fear
Of darkness, uppercuts, stab wounds and missing kidneys
Until you came
In a flared vase turtleneck,
A head of messy flowers
Platform heels that clocked like hooves
And when we held hands
Walford became lavender.

Five years later I told you that Walford
Came to Bombay. Outside Churchgate
I turned and there it was but not you.
You laughed- it was the perfume you'd always used.
We played the same game-
Turtleneck, messy head, platform heels
And when you fell in my arms-
'Like hugging a familiar blanket', you said
You smelt like a flower but nothing like Walford.

Ganeshguri

Two months after they autobot-ed
A bus-stand into a bookshelf
It's again the same coming

And going: late buses, ditched sandals
Early rains and dried ketchup.
This Ganeshguri morning

An ancient tree shrugs
Last night's piss.
A haunted espresso machine

In a knockoff Coffee Day
Sputters as you turn away
From a moth with sandpaper wings

And search the petrol pump
Tyre shops, rickshaw stand
For a little air

At six thirty you turn around
As you do after Eid prayers
Back home through an un-walked path

Begging to fill
The emptiness sagging
Your tyres

For home is not where
But when one returns
After trying everything.

Jalukbari

Just before Guwahati
Where buses fly over the river
on anew rainbow

I look out
And they are all there
Under the udders
Of the rainbow

They could be new believers
Their gospel on the walls,
Their rightful place under the rainbow

Edict number one- 'Foreigners not welcome'

Or as it is, they could be lynching
A new rose for the rainbow

Lightning strikes
I wait
But under this window

There's no clap, even the pattering
The pitter-pattering is wheels
Sharpening gravel on the rainbow

What then, a peaceful protest
A public meeting? Ah
I get it! This rainbow is

Just a shelter from the rain.

What a thing the City is

Says Hasmat Ali,

You can buy the sky here.

And we nod over his betelnut box

As tentacles of these new Babels rise

Before our eyes.

What is it in this red soil of Guwahati, asks Ali

That feeds these things?

All around us the village

His grandma brought as dowry

Shrinks into a lone bitter gourd creeper among the terrace grills

A sparrow sits on the fingers of the parapet.

One day, says Hasmat Ali,

They will buy his handful of sky.

Ghost in my Kitchen

I know of the ghost in my kitchen
But do everything to convince myself otherwise.
There's no reason really
To ignore cutlery falling off shelves
Taps dripping in the middle of the night
And polythene bags
Scuttling along the marble

I blame rats, cockroaches, the breeze-
None of you have given me reason to complain
Except Mr. Rat who before I threw a sandal at him
Started humming Robert Plant
His arms gathered at his chest.
His little teeth trembled and his nose
Turned to his ancestors.

In a room dug deep in a hill
Where nights are not for sleeping
Where days slink into my coffee pot
Drip by drip
I hold myself guilty
For turning a blind eye to a child ghost
And depriving the world of
An immigrant rat.

White Bitch

You white bitch that spread
Your tits under the eucalyptus,
Where are your babies now?
A year ago I walked past
And you, heavy and immobile, drew a sheet of
Dried leaves over your breasts.
Where are your babies now?

And who was their father?
I saw one sailing on a rickshaw
In the floods last August.
The rain passed a watery rope through the wheels
And bound it to the street.
He slept and dreamt of Picasso,
His head on the handlebars,
His feet on the roof.
And you lifted a hand
And parted the curtains of rain
And looked at him.
Was it he?

Or was it he that peeked at you through the eyes of a Skoda?
The bags of chips, cashew nuts, livers of chicken,
Splashes of urine-
Were they flags he planted every night?
With the flag of love he planted in you?

Or were you seeded by the eucalyptus?
Did he chooseleaves from his hair and
In cleangreen cones, pack his sperm
And did you, obligingly
Bend your head and let the

Packets unwind in descent
And shower on you?
And when the babies bit their way out of your cunt
Did they pirouette upwards in pink tutus
And stick to their father as March blossoms?

Or did they waddle out happily into the road and
The Skoda, bloody at betrayal,
Drive vengeance over them,
Cracking their teeth,
Blackening their eyes,
Crunching their skulls?

Or did they just sniff at the red pavement
And piling the stink on their backs,
Simply walk away?

God's Gift to Advertising

I am Arun
Says the poet
And drops the mic.

The Ecstatic Woman stares in shock.

He walks down the aisle
One hand on a handlebar
One counting matchsticks in his pocket

The box has split
Across its face in permanent black
'Turnaround Bar, Colaba'

He orders a Kingfisher strong
And whispers to the froth,
'Write a bloody poem called beer.
Make it bloody.'

National Poet

Perhaps it was fitting that the national poet
Peeing by the slope
While returning from a failed performance
And unloading himself on a new lover
On a newly repaired phone
Should slip on his piss and take a fall

For who should take so disgraceful a fall
For failing an audience if not the poet?
And what if not a love-licked smart-phone
Should lead a heart up a slope,
Breathe down the lover
And light up at the performance?

A silent flailing, a hushed scrambling performance
It was; the friend, also peeing, oblivious to the fall
Heard the loud concern of the lover
And the pained cooing of the poet
Wondered if poetry had vanished from the slope,
Then saw in the bushes, the glimmer on the phone

'Did you fall man?' 'Hurt' said the phone
Love didn't fuse the lovers, it was the fall
Misfortune had danced in leotards at the performance
And now it was dancing, dick out, on the slope
'No poetry after debauchery', the poet
Said then. Now he only groaned to his lover.

'Help us up', hissed the lover
The friend dropped his hand to the phone
But he was six feet under, the poet-
An anti-climax to an anti-climax that was the performance

A fall from grace, then a real fall
A stage he was booed down from and now his silent cries by
the slope

The friend looks for a path down the slope
But hey, in his ear the whisper of the lover
At his waist a waist fresh from a fall
On his shoulder the blinking phone
And as proof that he lives to perform one more romance
'Baby I am good', says the limping poet

The driver hears about the fall, checks for cracks on the
phone,
Then rear-views the slope: 'Only a fucking drunk can survive
such a performance'
He says. The cracked voice of the lover checks for cracks on
the poet.

The Heart-Breaking Loneliness

Of an Indian bachelor
Is manifest in a single
Fish scale on his bed

That sets him thinking
And shaking a blanket
That marinates in only his farts

No more, just this one.

Did he fry
The fish with scales on,
Then spit them out

Or while taking a curved
Knife to the gut did
An unpaired contact lens

Break from the armour
And fly off-trajectory?
But it was *tengra*,

He remembers-
Fish with no scales.
He dwells on the privilege

Of meditative thought.
His breaks like a borali on ice
Not into small bones

But right down the centre
Along the spine.

Pig Men

Every May when the pig men came
Roads dried, windows overflowed
Embankment to market became a bed of cotton
And the air beaten clouds

First a mirage, then the thump of canes
Then the buzzing of pigs, thick as flies
In a swish of turbans, sweat and langots,
The compulsive seduction of haraam.

Haraam marched through arum, madar, datura, mud
The undergrowth chewed, the village emerged
And when an eel took their spears through the face,
Water beetles screamed nauzubillah and ran.

The embankment is metalled kaaba black
The annual purge of pig men done.
A holy village here
And the same story everywhere

Or maybe somewhere every May a village is born.

Udit Narayan

Follow the instructions for full effect:

1. April showers, Guwahati:
    buy meat, cook meat
    loosen buttons
    eat meat.

2. Your clothes are damp, the petunias are dead
    but it's alright.
    Peace seeks a seat on your eyelids
    then slowly spreads it legs and
    elbows out your soul-
    the poor thing waits at the platform for
    a train to Kotdwara
    The hands, in a clean deep pan
    boil milk.

3. After this it's all pretty simple:
    cardamoms, coconut cubes
    a little ginger, rice.
    Don't add sugar
    or linger too long in the bathroom-
    The train guard will knock for a fifty
    (or a thousand when he knows what you are up to).

4. Rice cooks
    milk thickens
    add sugar
    let it cool
    until the chilly sawdusty air
    at Kotdwara
    forces you into a taxi to Landsdowne.

Relax, watch the last live pines fly.

5.   Kheer is always torn
between tongue and spoon
but what do you care?
While white stain on spoon
And sweet cream on tongue draw their own truce,

Hum...

...and the buzzing in your throat,
the megaphone at the station,
the guard's pocket radio,
the taxi driver's cassette player will
all tempt back your soul
In the voice of Udit Narayan.

Crow

Few things inspire more confidence
Than crow on a garbage bin with
A piece of fish in his mouth-
Not just fish but a cleaned, perfectly
Cubed piece of *bhokua* stolen from
The butcher's guillotine
Or caught deftly when it flew off the slab
Not just a garbage bin, mind you
But fifty kilograms of metal
And the confidence!
If you make a sudden move, he may pick
Fish and garbage bin and fly.

Simal Tree

A simal declared my father old
I'll never forgive that simal tree
He parked his cycle against its trunk
And stood: too tired to ride, too dignified to squat.

I'll never forgive that simal tree
He picked a matchstick, one end rolled in cotton
And stood: too tired to ride, too dignified to squat
My father dug pus out of his ear

He picked a matchstick, one end rolled in cotton
And the simal pods popped
My father dug pus out of his ear
The street became a cotton field

Simal pods popped
Simal declared my father old
The street became a cotton field
His parked bicycle slid down the trunk.

Death by Music

If he doesn't listen to advice,
Keeps his headphones on while crossing
The road to Kay M Plaza
And is finally hit by a bus
Remove the four packets of Kamala Pasand from his pocket.
His mother should not know that
He has shifted to inferior gutkha.

Find two new photo albums in his bag-
One for boarding passes, one for
Handwritten copies of sms'es-
An idiotic love from a time before smartphones.
Hide the hole on his right shoe
Don't tell anyone that his left leg was stronger
And the right just dragged itself.

If he didn't bathe in the morning chances are
His head stinks of henna leaves fried in mustard oil
Cover his expanding bald spot.
And for God's sake don't reveal
The combination to the hidden folder
On his mobile phone.

Acknowledgments

Many thanks to those who are characters in this book. Some of them have been named, some names have been changed (for good reasons) and some are too long deceased to care.

My thanks to my brother Gulam Sarowar Hussain who read most of these poems in their early drafts and never offered a single word of advice.

Sister Nirmala Matthew, Mr. Ranjit Roy, Mr. Pradip Debnath, Ms. Mahua Sen and Ms. Moushumi taught me English. I thank them for giving me this language.

My sincere thanks to Linda Ashok, Mr. Robert Archambeau and the team of RL Poetry Award 2017 for the love they have shown this book. I hope we get to meet in person soon.

Many thanks to Ms. Teresa Rehman for drawing me back into poetry.

In 2010, Ms. Jayashree Borthakur gifted me a laptop computer on which most of these poems were written. I can never repay that debt.

And finally my thanks to Guwahati, the *Betelnut City*, for helping me discover youth.